PIANO • VOCAL • GUITAR

KATHY MATTEA

Good News

D0123232

Photography: McGuire

ISBN 0-7935-3715-0

HAL•LEONARD CORPORATION
7777 W. Bluemound Rd. P.O. Box 13819 Milwaukee, WI 53213

W9-CHF-878

KATHY MATTEA

GOOD NEWS

BRIGHTEST AND BEST

Adapted and Arranged by KATHY MATTEA
and BRENT MAHER

Dm
C/D
Dm
Lo for a God the bright an - gels at - tend.
Wise men and shep - herds be - fore Him do fall.
Solo ends
G
Bright - est and best of sons of the morn - ing,
mf
Dm
G
A
Dm
dawn on our dark - ness and lend us thine aid. Star in the East, the hor - i -
mp
C/D
Dm
To Coda
1
C/D
- zon a - dorn - ing, guide where our in - fant Re - deem - er was

Dm
C/D
laid.
8va
loco
8va
Dm
loco
8va
loco
2
D.S. al Coda
C/D
Dm
deem - er was laid.
CODA
C/D
Dm
deem - er was laid.
8va
C
Dm
loco
8va
loco
8va
loco

EMMANUEL

Words and Music by JANIS IAN
and KYE FLEMING

*This can be sung as a 3 part round, with the 2nd and 3rd voices entering at these places.

F
Bb
1
F
Bb
Joy to all the world this night. And to all _ peo-ple, peace. And to all _ peo-ple, peace. Re -
2
Bb
F
Bb
to all _ peo-ple peace. Em - man - u - el, Em - man - u - el. A
child is born. A child is born. Sing glo - ry un - to God on high.
F
Bb
F
Bb
Repeat and Fade
Joy to all the world this night. And to all _ peo-ple, peace. And to all _ peo-ple peace. Em -

CHRIST CHILD'S LULLABYE

Adapted and Arranged by KATHY MATTEA
and DOUGIE MacLEAN
Translation by KENNA CAMPBELL

B♭
Gm
3fr
love - ly son are you. You
heart with which you came. A
Son, E - ter - nal One. You
C
B♭
are my love my dar - ling
ten - der, help - less ti - ny
are my God and help - less
C
B♭
new. Un - wor - thy I of
babe with bound - less gifts of
son, High Rul - er of Man -
F
C
you.
grace.
kind.
Al -

B♭
C
le - lu - ia,
B♭
al - le - lu -
Gm
3 fr
C
ia, al - le -
B♭
C
lu - ia, al - le -

B♭
To Coda
F
1
lu
-
ia.
Your
2
Am7
Em7
Am7
Em7

B♭
D.S. al Coda
CODA
F
ia.
C
B♭
Al - le - lu -
C
B♭
ia, al - le -

Gm
3fr
C
lu - ia, al -
B♭
C
le - lu - ia, al -
B♭
F
le - lu - ia.
1
2

GOOD NEWS

Words, Music and Choral Arrangement by
ROB MATHES

C7
F
B♭sus/C
B♭
leave you with Good News.
B♭5
B♭m
F/A
Close your eyes, fold your hands, for a
Bow your head, speak not a word, let the
3
Fm(add4)/A♭
3fr
G♭maj7
mo - ment let your sor - row fade.
si - lence take you far from here.

Fsus
F/A
B♭m
Fm(add4)/A♭
3fr
Why? Oh why are you a - fraid?
The spi - rit of a child dry ev - 'ry tear
E♭m/G♭
E♭m7
F/A
Gm7
3fr
F
F/A
B♭m
3
Has this world stripped you of your Faith?
and may your doubts they dis - ap - pear.
Close your eyes and on
Bow your head and on
F/D♭
Fm(add4)/A♭
3fr
bend - ed knee,
bend - ed knee,
lis - ten to an an - gel
hear the sto - ry once a -
G♭maj7
F
F7/A
3fr
B♭m
Fm(add4)/A♭
3fr
pray,
gain.
and once a - gain pre - pare the way,
The child grew up to wear a cross,

Ebm/Gb Eb/G Ab Ab/Gb Db Gb/Db
so you'll see a gift that's given. For you, a
the child grew up to pledge a life. For us a
Db7 Gb/Db Fsus F Bb Dm7
time of joy. Be - hold a ba - by boy.
time of joy. Be - hold Christ a ba - by boy.
Good
Eb F Bb
News, Good News,
Gm7 C C/E F Bb/D Eb F/Bb
an An - gel brings Good News. Good

Eb Fm Eb/G Eb Bb/F D/F# Gm
News, Good News,
D7/A D7 Gm7 C7 F
To Coda
I leave you with Good
Bb5
1 2
News.
Bbm F/A
For us His on - ly Son, in a

Fm(add4)/A♭
3fr
G♭maj7
man - ger wrapped in swad - dling clothes, ___
F
F/A
B♭m
Fm(add4)/A♭
3fr
E♭m/G♭
E♭/G
3fr
Christ the Sav - ior, Christ-mas Day,
all our bur - dens washed a -
A♭
4fr
A♭/G♭
4fr
D♭
G♭/D♭
4fr
D♭7
4fr
D♭
way.
We break the bread, we pour the
G♭
Cm7♭5
wine ___
and an an - gel de -

D.S. al Coda
Bbm/F F Bb Dm7
scends with a heav - en - ly sign. Good
CODA
Bb5 Bb Dm7
News. Good
Eb Fm Eb/G Eb F Bb
News. Good News,
3fr
Gm7 C C/E F Bb/D Eb F/Bb
an An - gel brings Good News. Good

Eb
Fm
Eb/G
Eb
Bb/F
D/F#
Gm
3fr
News, Good News,
D7/A
D7
Gm7
C7
F
I bring you,
C7
F
no chord
an An - gel brings Good (Good,
Bb
Good) News.

MARY, DID YOU KNOW?

Words and Music by MARK LOWRY
and BUDDY GREENE

F♯m E Bm7 2fr
know that your ba - by boy would save our sons and daugh -
know that your ba - by boy will calm a storm with his
know that your ba - by boy will one day rule the na -
C♯7sus C♯7 Bm7 2fr E
- ters? Did you know that your ba - by boy has
hand? Did you know that your ba - by boy has
- tions? Did you know that your ba - by boy was
mf
A E/G♯ F♯m Bm7 2fr
To Coda
come to make you new? This child that you've de - liv -
walked where an - gels trod? When you've kissed your lit - tle ba -
Heav - en's per - fect Lamb? This sleep - ing child you're hold -
C♯7sus
1
C♯7
- ered will soon de - liv - er you. Mar - y, did you
- by, then you've kissed the face of God.
dim.
mp

2
C#7
F#m
E
mp
Bm7
2fr
C#7sus
C#7
F#m
Mar - y, did you know?
3
E
Bm7
2fr
C#7sus
C#7
Mar - y, did you know? _ The blind_
3
3
mf
D
E
F#m
E
_ will see, _ the deaf _ will hear, _ the dead _ will live _ a - gain. _

D
Bm7
2 fr
E
The lame will leap, the dumb will speak the prais-
F♯m
C♯7sus
C♯7
D.S. al Coda
- es of the Lamb. Mar - y, did you
CODA
C♯7sus
C♯7
- ing is the great "I
cresc.
F♯m
E
Bm7
2 fr
C♯7
F♯m
Am."
mf
molto rit. e dim.
p

SOMEBODY TALKIN' ABOUT JESUS

Adapted and Arranged by KATHY MATTEA
and BRENT MAHER

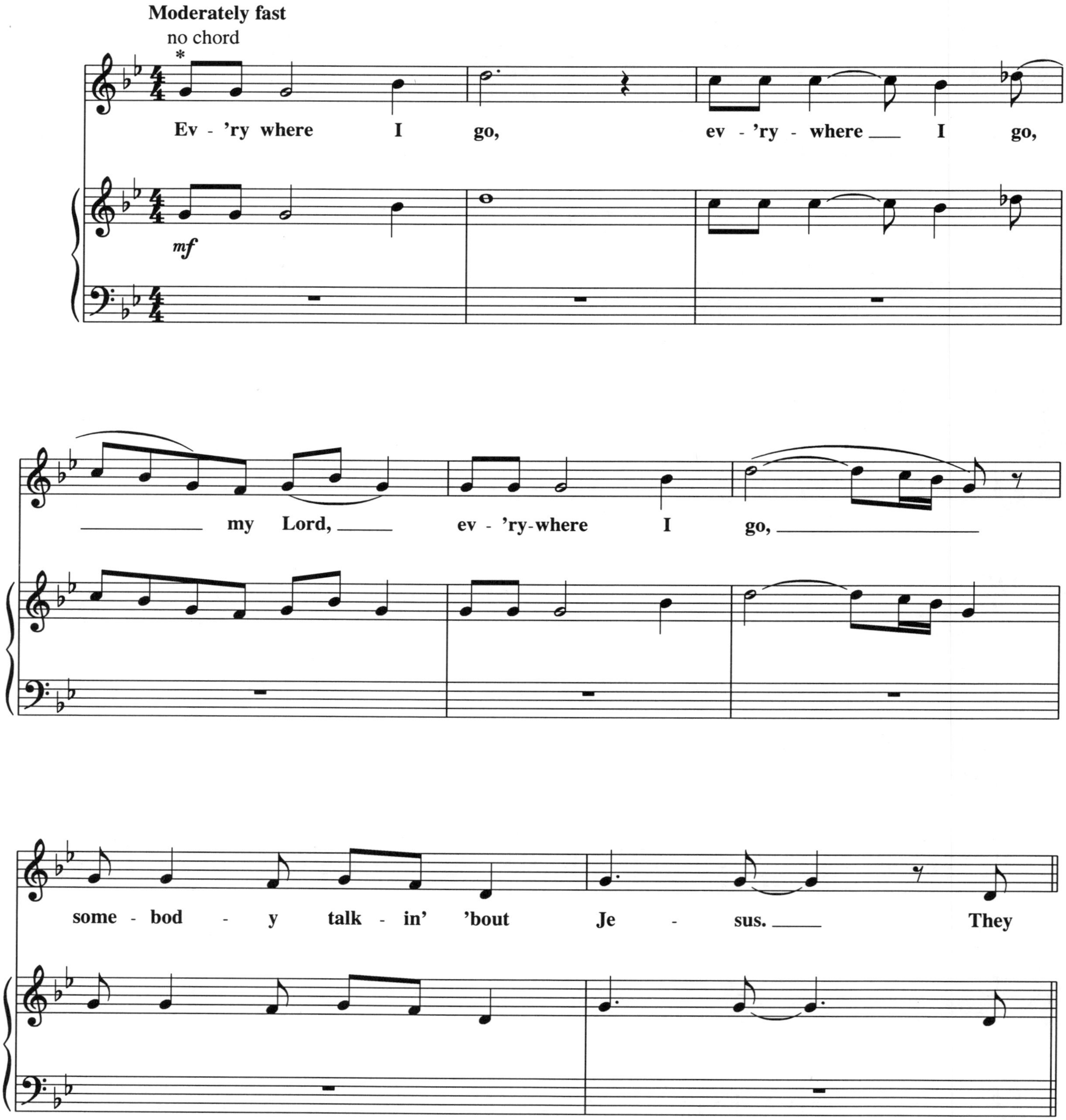

*Vocal written an octave higher than sung.

Gm
3fr
C
Gm
3fr
C
turned a - way ___ Mar - y and Jo - seph from the Inn.
Born, born of the Vir - gin Mar - y.
Gm
3fr
C
Gm
3fr
C
Some - bod - y talk - in' 'bout Je - sus. ___ A ba - by born in
Some - bod - y talk - in' 'bout Je - sus. ___ Born, born on
Gm
3fr
C
Gm
3fr
E♭
3fr
Gm/D
D7
Beth - le - hem. ___ Some - bod - y talk - in' 'bout Je - sus. ___
Christ - mas Morn. _ Some - bod - y talk - in' 'bout Je - sus. ___
Gm
3fr
Cm
3fr
Ev - 'ry - where I go, ev - 'ry - where ___ I go, _

Am7♭5
D7
Gm
3fr
To Coda
my Lord,
ev - 'ry - where
I
go,
Eb
3fr
D7
Gm
3fr
C
some - bod - y talk - in' 'bout
Je - sus.
Gm
3fr
Cm
3fr
Guitar solo
Am7♭5
D7
Gm
3fr

D
Gm
3fr
Gm
C
Gm
C
Glo - ry be to the New - born Babe.
Gm
C
D.S. al Coda
Some - bod - y talk - in' 'bout Je - sus. Oh.
CODA
E♭
Am7♭5
D
Gm
some - bod - y talk - in' 'bout Je - sus.
rit.

THE STAR

Words and Music by
PETER McCANN

C♯m7
4fr
F♯m
Bm7
2fr
Esus
E
un - der - neath the star so far a - way.
in - to ev - 'ry heart so tired and torn.
born be - neath the star so long a - go.
1
A
D/E
She car-ried ev - 'ry-thing
2,3
D/A
A
And the light
cresc.
D
A
E7
shin - ing from that star will show you who you are.
mf
A
D
And His light shin-ing with its might will

A/E
To Coda
lead you through the dark - est night.
dim.
E
D/E
D.S. al Coda (take 2nd ending)
They could-n't find a room
mp
CODA
E
D/E
Just an-oth - er home -
mp
A
E/G♯
A
E/B
- less fam - i - ly,
hop-ing for a strang -
A/C♯
Bm7
2 fr
E7
A
A/C♯
- er's char - i - ty,
just one night in one

D
E
C♯m7
4fr
F♯m
safe place to stay,
un - der - neath the star
Bm7
2fr
Esus
E
A
E7/B
so far a - way.
A/C♯
D
Bm7
2fr
A/C♯
D
Esus
E
A(add2)
rit.

THERE'S A NEW KID IN TOWN

Words and Music by CURLY PUTMAN,
DON COOK and KEITH WHITLEY

Smoothly

fol - low - ing the star,
shin - ing
say these gifts are for
the new King's
F/C
C
G
Am
C/G
bright - er.
Old man, won't you
pleas - ures.
I've heard
Fmaj7
Dm7
help us if you can?
He shook his head
but he
that a King might come,
but up 'til now there
has - n't
Fmaj7
G
C
point - ed his hand.
been one.
There's a new kid in town,

Em7
F
C
and He's ly - ing in a man - ger down the road. There's a
Em7
F
new kid in town, but He's just an - oth - er ba - by, I sup - pose.
Am
D7
F
To Coda
Heav - en knows there's a new kid in town,
1
F/G
C
F/C
C
here in Beth - le - hem.

G7
C
I
2
F/G
C
D.S al Coda
F/G
G
F/G
G
here in Beth- le - hem.
There's a
CODA
F/G
C
F/C
C
here in Beth - le - hem.
G/B
Am
F
C
molto rit.

WHAT A WONDERFUL BEGINNING

Words and Music by AUSTIN CUNNINGHAM
and ALLEN SHAMBLIN

MCA music publishing

Smoothly, flowing
mp
F
Oh, the an - gels were re - joic - ing as the ti - ny ba - by cried. For the
won - der - ful be - gin - ning to the great - est sto - ry ev - er told. His
Bb/F
F
Bb/F
F
hope of man's sal - va - tion in a man - ger had ar - rived.
birth still rings with prom - ise as true as in days of old.
Bb
F/A
Gm7
3 fr
F
C/E
F
Meek as a low - ly shep - herd but the
So let us sing His prais - es and let us

Bb/F
F
Bb/F
might - i - est of kings, He gives peace and life e -
o - pen up our hearts, and re - ceive His time - less
F
Bb/F
F
C/E
F
ter - nal to who - so - ev - er calls His name.
mes - sage that gives us all a brand new start.
poco rit.
Slower
C/E
Bb/D
F/C
Bb
F
Oh, Em - man - u - el, the Fa - ther's pre - cious
mf
Dm
C/E
F
C/E
Bb
F
Son, who for - gives our sins and wash - es clean the

Bb/F C/E
1 F Bb/F F Bb/F C/E F Bb/F F
Tempo I
hearts of ev - 'ry one. What a
2 F Bb/F F
Freely
Bb F C Dm
one. Oh, a man named John The Bap - tist had been
Bb F C Bb F C Dm
her - ald - ing the news a-bout the com - ing of a Sav - ior for both the
Bb F C F
Gen - tiles and the Jews.

NOTHING BUT A CHILD

Words and Music by
STEVE EARLE

G6
Songs of praise to sing, they travelled day and night.
scarce be-lieved their eyes. They'd come so man-y miles.
ev-'ry moth-er, kind and ev-'ry fa-ther, proud,
A/C♯
G
A/C♯
Pre-cious gifts to bring, they were guid-
The mir-a-cle they prized was noth-
looks down in awe to find an-oth-
G
A7
1
D
2,3
D
-ed by the light. They
-ing but a child.
-er chance al-lowed.
G
D
G6
D
A/C♯
Noth-ing but a child could wash those tears a-way

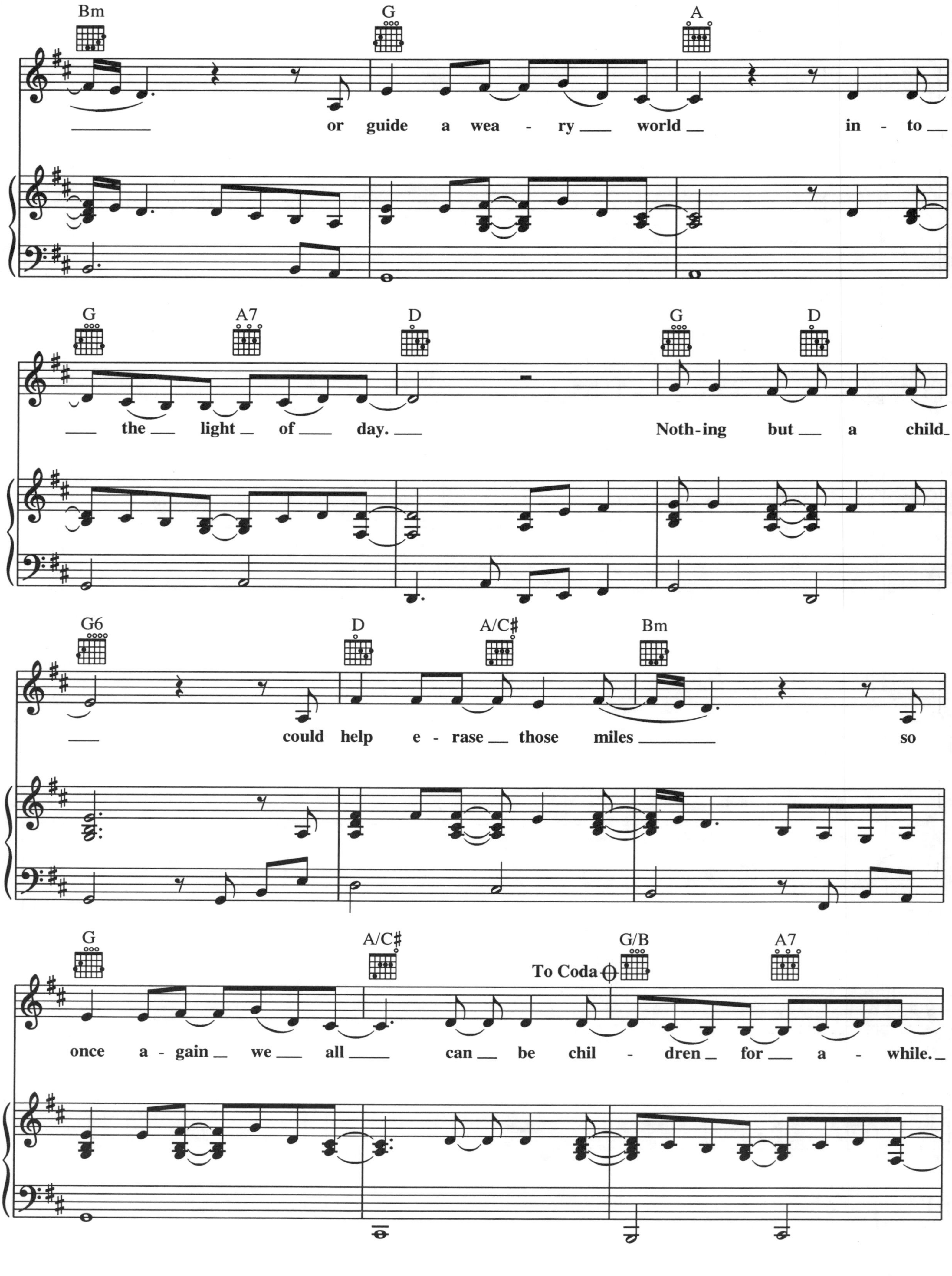
Bm G A
or guide a wea - ry world in - to
G A7 D G D
the light of day. Noth-ing but a child
G6 D A/C# Bm
could help e - rase those miles so
G A/C# To Coda G/B A7
once a - gain we all can be chil - dren for a - while.

D
G
A/C♯
G
A/C♯
Em7
A7
D
D.S. al Coda
(take 2nd ending)
Now
CODA
G/B
A7/C♯
D
- dren for a - while.
3

G
Noth - ing but a lit -
A/C♯
G
- tle ba - by. Noth - ing but a lit -
A
G/B
A7/C♯
- tle ba - by. Noth - ing but a child.
D
rit.